The FABULOUS FLYING MACHINES of ALBERTO SANTOS-DUMONT

VICTORIA GRIFFITH

Illustrations by
EVA MONTANARI

Abrams Books for Young Readers · New York

Alberto Santos-Dumont loved floating over Paris in his own personal flying machine. It had helped make him one of the most famous men in the city, if not the world! *Everyone,* he thought, *should have this much fun running a simple errand.*

On a sunny summer afternoon in 1903, the Brazilian had taken his airship out for some shopping. Alberto flew over a sea of horse-drawn carriages. Then he spotted an automobile just ahead. Flying low enough to shout to the car's driver, Alberto cried out, "I'll race you to the park!" The race was on. He pulled on a lever to speed up. The car didn't have a chance and Alberto congratulated himself as his dirigible—a controllable balloon of his own design—glided effortlessly past the car and to the finish line. His airship was truly the best way to get around.

Pulling on a cord to let air out of the balloon, Alberto began his descent. A long rope hanging down from the dirigible dragged along the street. A snapping dog ran angrily after it. The doorman of the hat shop, used to Alberto's unusual choice of transportation, rushed forward to take the rope and tie it to a post. While Alberto shopped, the doorman would make sure the airship didn't float away.

A crowd gathered around, excited to see the handsome Brazilian in person. "One day you'll all have a flying machine!" he called out.

"Take me up with you!" cried a pretty young woman from the crowd. She knew from stories in the newspapers that Alberto sometimes offered rides to complete strangers.

"Another time," Alberto replied regretfully. "Right now, I need a new hat. Sadly, my last one was burned beyond repair." The hydrogen gas that made the airship float had an unfortunate tendency to catch fire, and Alberto often used his hats to quench the flames. These mishaps made him a frequent customer at the hat shop.

Inside, the store's attendant handed Alberto a new straw hat and listened to him talk about how flight would change the world. "I tell you," said Alberto, placing the hat on his head, "these machines will mean the end of all wars. Once people are able to fly to different countries, they will see how much we have in common. We will all be friends."

"I hope you are right, Monsieur," smiled the attendant.

A few minutes later, Alberto climbed back into the basket of his airship. His next stop was the fashionable Maxim's restaurant, where he would share a coffee with his friend Louis Cartier. Louis was an inventor too, of pocket watches and jewelry. A couple of years earlier, Alberto had complained to his friend that he was unable to pull out his pocket watch during flight, because his hands were so busy with the controls. Louis had promised to come up with a solution.

This time, when Alberto reached the skies, the winds were blowing against him. It slowed him down, and he arrived at Maxim's a little behind schedule.

"You're late!" said Louis in a teasing voice as Alberto joined him. "By five minutes and thirty-three seconds, to be precise." As a watchmaker, Louis was obsessed with time.

"I'm sorry," Alberto apologized. He didn't want to admit that a small breeze had slowed him down. "But as you know, I can't check my pocket watch up in the air."

"Yes, I know," Louis said. "I promised to find a solution to your watch problem. Well, it's taken me some time, but at last I have come up with something." He handed Alberto a box.

Alberto opened it, burning with curiosity.

"It's a wristwatch," Louis explained.

At parties, Alberto had seen aristocratic ladies wearing chains on their wrists with tiny watches attached. They didn't look very practical—the clock faces were too small, the chains too delicate. The watch Louis had just given him was very different. It looked sturdy, with a square clock face. On the top and bottom, the watch was attached to thick leather straps. Alberto put it on and gazed at it with admiration. He was touched. "I'll put it to good use," Alberto promised. "Remember when I flew around the Eiffel Tower for that big prize? I had to do it in twenty-nine minutes! I wasn't even sure I'd won, because I couldn't check the time. Now, I'll know how quickly I'm moving, and it will be more important than ever. I've made a decision. It's fun hopping around Paris, but for flight to be truly useful, I need to go farther and faster."

"But your dirigible has made you one of the most famous people in the world! Why take a chance on something else?"

"Even the best invention can be improved," Alberto said. "You've shown me that with this new wristwatch."

Alberto worked hard on his new invention for three years. On a chilly November morning in 1906, Louis Cartier drove eagerly in his automobile to a field just outside of Paris.

Alberto had promised something new and exciting, and Louis wouldn't miss it for the world.

As he drew near, Louis couldn't believe his
eyes. Nearly a thousand people were crowded
onto the grass. Could Alberto's new flying
machine be this important?

In the middle of the field sat Alberto's invention. It looked like
a funny kite, but Louis recognized it as something called an airplane. Engineers had been building them for years without being
able to get them off the ground. Suddenly, Louis understood why
so many people had come. They believed Alberto could succeed
where so many others had failed.

But Alberto's airplane was not the only one on the field. There was another, sleeker machine in the distance. Louis knew the man standing beside it. It was another Louis—Louis Blériot, who bragged that he, not Alberto, would be the first to fly a plane.

"What's going on?" Louis Cartier asked someone in the crowd as he stepped out of his car.

"Blériot heard Santos would try to fly today and showed up uninvited," said the man. "He says he's not going to let Santos get the credit for inventing the airplane. He's going to fly his machine too. Everyone's wondering what Santos will do."

Alberto was already walking toward his rival. Would he tell Blériot to go home? Would there be a fight? The spectators were more silent than anyone would expect. Then, a murmur went through the crowd.

"Unbelievable!" shouted a man near Louis.

"What did Santos say?" asked Louis.

"He said—'Perhaps Monsieur would care to go first?'! Well, Santos is a gentleman, I'll say that, but he'll pay a high price for it." Louis drew in his breath. The man was right. This was not the moment for good manners. If Blériot succeeded to fly first, everyone would call him the inventor of the airplane.

Blériot was already climbing into the cockpit.
He started the engine and moved down the field,
faster and faster. The machine strained and wheezed
but remained firmly on the ground. Blériot
returned to the starting point to try again. Once
more, he failed to take off. Alberto watched calmly,
sipping a cup of coffee. On the third attempt, Blériot
ran out of chances. Instead of rising in the air, his
plane fell apart! Now it was Alberto's turn.

Alberto started his engine. The airplane moved down the field in a burst of energy. The cheering crowd raced after it. The airplane was going fast. Would it fly, or would it fall apart like Blériot's? Everyone watched as the wheels lifted just off the ground.

For a moment, it seemed the airplane would come back down to Earth with a thud. Instead, it pushed into the sky until it was soaring over the heads of the spectators. Higher and higher it went. Alberto turned around in the air and headed back.

Now, people scattered to avoid being hit by the plane, which was descending fast.

It was a hard landing. One of the wings broke, and a wheel twisted. It didn't matter. Alberto had become the first man to take off in a plane using its own power!

The cheers were deafening. Alberto climbed down from the cockpit, and was lifted on the shoulders of delirious fans. Louis pressed closer, but there were too many people around for him to get near Alberto. Then, he caught his friend's eye. Alberto looked at Louis, and pointed happily to his wrist. He was wearing the Cartier watch.

"Twenty-one seconds!" everyone was shouting. Alberto had gone fast, faster than his dirigible, fast enough to conquer the wind. And he had marked the time in the air on his own wristwatch.

"No one will ever forget this day!" shouted a man in the crowd. Reporters rushed off to write their stories. The next morning, Alberto and his airplane would be on the front page of every newspaper in the world!

Louis shook his head in wonder. He had given his friend a small present. Alberto had repaid him and the world with a far more precious gift—the gift of flight. Would it bring about the peace that Alberto dreamed of? Louis wasn't sure, but he knew the airplane would change the world forever. *Yes,* Louis thought, *this is a day that will never be forgotten.*

Alberto Santos-Dumont, circa 1906.

AUTHOR'S NOTE

"When the names of those who have occupied outstanding positions in the world have been forgotten, there will be a name which will remain in our memory, that of Santos-Dumont," said the *London Times* in 1901.

Years later I asked my daughter Sophia, "What did you learn in school today?"

"We learned how the Wright Brothers invented the airplane," she answered. It was an unremarkable response to an unremarkable question.

So I was unprepared for my Brazilian husband's reaction. "That's ridiculous!" he exclaimed, horrified. "Everyone knows that Alberto Santos-Dumont invented the airplane."

I was intrigued. During the years we lived in Brazil, I had heard Santos-Dumont referred to as the "Father of Flight." Yet I had not completely absorbed the depth of disagreement over who deserved credit for the first airplane. I decided to find out more and discovered that the claim to the invention remains controversial.

Orville and Wilbur Wright flew their airplane in December 1903 in front of a handful of witnesses. Yet the airplane needed assistance to get off the ground. The Wrights depended on high winds, as well as a rail system that propelled the plane forward. Critics argue that to count as a true airplane, a machine needs to take off with its own power.

While the Wright Brothers were soaring over Kitty Hawk, a dapper Brazilian called Alberto Santos-Dumont (1873–1932) was making his own mark on history. Santos-Dumont was a larger-than-life character. He was born on a Brazilian coffee plantation, where he devoured the science-fiction books of Jules Verne and showed an early mechanical talent. Henrique, his father, modernized the plantation with up-to-date machinery and became extremely wealthy.

After falling from a horse in 1891, Henrique was partially paralyzed. In search of a cure, the coffee magnate moved his family to Paris. There, Santos-Dumont took his first balloon ride. He was immediately hooked, and would spend most of his life—and much of his considerable fortune—pursuing the dream of controllable flight.

Alberto possessed that remarkable, if ephemeral, thing called "star quality." At the height of his career, he was one of the most famous men in the world. Children played with toy models of his airships. Bakers decorated their pastries with the colors of the Brazilian flag in his honor. On a trip to the United States, Alberto lunched with inventor Thomas Edison and President Theodore Roosevelt.

The flamboyant Alberto was the only man ever known to use a dirigible—a steerable, motorized balloon—to run everyday errands. He parked his 35-foot airship in front of his apartment building on the Champs-Élysées and took it out to go shopping or to pay visits to friends. Alberto sometimes tethered his flying machine to a lamppost in front of a fashionable café and asked the waiters to send him up a glass of champagne or coffee.

In 1901, Alberto rode his dirigible around the Eiffel Tower and back to a park just outside of central Paris in twenty-nine minutes. For that feat, he was awarded 100,000 francs in prize money. Always generous, he gave half to his workmen, and the other half to Paris' poor.

Alberto often complained to his friend, the jeweler Louis Cartier, that he couldn't keep track of the time when flying. Because he needed both hands to steer the craft, he was unable to pull out his pocket watch. Cartier promised to come up with a solution. Sometime before Alberto's first airplane flight—historians are unsure of the exact date—he presented Alberto with the first men's wristwatch. Soon, men all over Europe were wearing one.

On November 12, 1906, three years after the Wright venture, Alberto Santos-Dumont drove to a field just outside of Paris to make what he promised would be the world's first public airplane flight. Nearly a thousand people showed up to witness the event. In a surprise to everyone, Louis Blériot (who would later become the first man to cross the English Channel in a plane) had brought his own flying machine and was determined to steal the show.

Santos-Dumont gallantly offered to let his rival try first. Blériot's plane, after three attempts, fell apart. Santos-Dumont seized the moment. He flew for little more than twenty seconds, but it was long enough to gain recognition as the first pilot to lift off and land a completely self-propelled airplane. Largely unaware of the Wright Brothers' flights a few years earlier, the entire world celebrated Alberto's accomplishment.

Orville and Wilbur Wright conducted their experiments in secrecy, because they were terrified that someone would steal their designs before they could make money from them. France did not see the Wright Brothers' plane until 1908, when the brothers went to Paris in search of a lucrative military contract. (When the Europeans did see the Wright Brothers fly, they were bowled over by the supreme control Orville and Wilbur demonstrated in flight.)

Alberto was an idealist. He never sought patents for his inventions and gave away most of the money he won from competitions. He thought his "flying machines" would bring about permanent world peace. He lived his final years in his native Brazil, suffering from what is believed now to have been multiple sclerosis. The world—outside of South America and France—forgot him with remarkable speed. In 1932, distraught over the use of his beloved flying machines for warfare, and bewildered by his abrupt fall from favor, sadly he took his own life.

Even without being credited with the first flight, Santos-Dumont deserves a place in history books. He invented the first practical dirigible, and went on to design the world's first mass-produced airplane, the *Dragonfly*. His airborne legend is now overshadowed by that of other flight pioneers. Yet his impact on fashion has remained intact. The Santos, as the model is still called, remains one of Cartier's best-selling wristwatches.

Alberto riding his dirigible around the Eiffel Tower. October 19, 1901.

Alberto was the first pilot to lift off and land a completely self-propelled plane.

SELECTED BIBLIOGRAPHY

Barros, Henrique Lins de. *Santos-Dumont and the Invention of the Airplane*. Rio de Janeiro: Brazilian Ministry of Science and Technology and the Brazilian Center for Research in Physics, 2006.

Downie, Andrew, "A Century On, Brazil Still Claims Flight's First," *Christian Science Monitor*, October 23, 2006.

Hoffman, Paul. *Wings of Madness*. New York: Hyperion, 2003.

Mattos, Bento de. "Santos-Dumont and the Dawn of Aviation." American Institute of Aeronautics and Astronautics /AIAA paper presented at the Aerospace Sciences Meeting and Exhibit, Reno, NV, January 2004.

Moura Visoni, Rodrigo. *Santos-Dumont and the Wright Brothers: End of the Century-Old Polemic*. Rio de Janeiro: Historical and Cultural Institute of the Brazilian Airforce/INCAER, 2006.

Santos-Dumont, Alberto. *My Airships*. New York: Dover Publications, 1973, orig. publ. 1904.

Winters, Nancy. *Man Flies: The Story of Alberto Santos-Dumont*. New York: Ecco Press, 1997.

www.santos-dumont.net

INDEX

ART NOTE

The illustrations in this book were created using pastels, chalks, oil pastels, and oil paint on simple (and sometimes recycled) colored paper.

For Vinicius, Sophia, and Isabel
—V. G.

A mia zia Clara dalle favolose creazioni…
(To my aunt Clara, who creates fabulous things…)
—E. M.

Library of Congress Cataloging-in-Publication Data

Griffith, Victoria.
The fabulous flying machines of Alberto Santos-Dumont / by Victoria Griffith ; illustrated by Eva Montanari.
p. cm.
Includes bibliographical references.
ISBN 978-1-4197-0011-8 (alk. paper)
1. Santos-Dumont, Alberto, 1873–1932—Juvenile literature.
2. Aeronautical engineers—Brazil—Biography—Juvenile literature. 3. Airplanes—History—Juvenile literature. 4. Aeronautics—History—Juvenile literature. 5. Airships—History—Juvenile literature. I. Montanari, Eva, 1977– ill. II. Title.
TL540.S25G73 2011
629.130092—dc22
[B]
2010048781

Text copyright © 2011 Victoria Griffith
Illustrations copyright © 2011 Eva Montanari
Book design by Maria T. Middleton
Photographers unknown.

THE ART OF BOOKS SINCE 1949
115 West 18th Street
New York, NY 10011
www.abramsbooks.com